ISBN: 979-8-234-04447-1

Scripture quotations, unless otherwise indicated, are taken from the *Holy Bible, King James Version and New International Version* of the Bible.

Published by:

Naveda Walker

Veda Consultants LLC

www.VedaWalker.com

Cover and graphic design by:

Naveda Walker

Investments By Faith LLC

www.InvestmentsByFaith.com

Published in the United States of America

CONTENTS

Rejected BUT Chosen

NAVEDA WALKER

Rejected. Abandoned. Betrayed.

Still, God saw you, chose you, and kept you.

No matter who mishandled you,

Jesus loves you.

No matter who abandoned you,

God is with you.

No matter who spoke against you,

the cross speaks for you.

You are not rejected—

you are *chosen*.

REJECTED
BUT
CHOSEN

The Author's Message for You

"God knows you."
"God sees you."

He knew you before He formed you in your mother's womb. You were not an accident, a mistake, or an afterthought. You were set apart, created with intention and purpose.

As it is written in **Jeremiah 1:5**:
"Before I formed you in the womb I knew you, before you were born, I set you apart."

You are called to be **better**.
You are called to be **greater**.

It may not seem like it right now. It may not feel like it, especially when the weight of pain and suffering feels heavy. But hear me clearly, you are **built for this**.

You were built to look different, sis.
You were built to look different, bro.

You are meant to be different, sound different, think different. To become better. To do better. To rise higher. Even to carry yourself differently because what God placed inside of you is not ordinary.

I share my story to give you **hope**, **strength**, and **clarity** to help you get up from that dark place.

Get up from that dark place, sis.
Get up from that dark place, bro.

If I survived it for you, then you can survive it for you and your family too.

I love you.
And most importantly **God loves you too**.

Introduction: *Rejected but Chosen*

I am living proof that God sees everything and knows everything we are facing. Nothing about your life is hidden from him. Your pain, your struggles, your mistakes, your questions, he knows them all.

Breakthrough and healing **are possible** if you truly desire change.

You may have lived a life full of sin, mistakes, or poor choices, but God is still willing to forgive you, love you, and walk with you. He is not the kind of God who leaves or abandons his children. He is faithful even when we have not been.

The Word of God reminds us in **Psalm 27:10**,
"Though my father and mother forsake me, the Lord will receive me."

God loves you, and He loves all of us as His children. However, just as a loving parent corrects their child, God also calls us to repentance. When a child gets in trouble, discipline may come but forgiveness always follows when there is accountability, repentance, and change.

So, it is with our Heavenly Father.
We must repent and turn away from sin. Not because God wants to punish us, but because he wants to **restore** us.

No matter what you have done whether it was murder, witchcraft, stealing, abortion, sexual sin, or any other wrongdoing there is still room at the altar for you. Go to your Heavenly Father. Repent sincerely.

Turn away from those ways. And choose not to return to them.

God promises us in **2 Chronicles 7:14,**
"If my people, who are called by my name, will humble themselves and pray and seek my face and turn from their wicked ways, then I will hear from heaven, and I will forgive their sin and will heal their land."

I was not perfect. And God was not pleased with everything I endured or participated in. But the moment I ran to Him, He covered me. He protected me. He kept me.

As written in **Psalm 91:1–4**, God provides refuge, safety, and covering to those who dwell in Him.

And He will keep you too.

There are promises that God has spoken over all of our lives, but many of us never experience them because we do not seek him or build a relationship with him. We cannot receive what we refuse to pursue.

2 Peter 1:4 reminds us that God has given us great and precious promises.
Psalm 105:4 instructs us to seek the Lord and His strength continually.

My testimony stands as proof that God is real.
And so are His promises.

Dr. Naveda Walker

Dedication

This book is dedicated to my brothers and sisters who share stories like mine.

I had to write this book as an act of obedience an assignment given to me by my Heavenly Father, Yahweh. This book was not written for entertainment; it was written for **freedom**. Freedom from loneliness, depression, suicidal thoughts, rejection, anxiety, fear, worry, and stress. Because the truth is we are not alone. It only feels that way when we don't realize we don't have to be.

I am here today to tell you that I **survived for you**.
I am still living for you.
I am still healing and growing for you.

I share my story to give you hope, to help you break free, and to introduce you to the God I know and serve the God who never left me, even when everyone else did. You are not alone.

Jesus reminds us in **Matthew 28:20**, *"And surely I am with you always, even to the end of the age."*

My name is **Naveda Walker**, and I want to remind you that God is always with you. When you feel like you have no one else, hold on to Him. You may not have a support system. You may not have real friends. You may not have family who shows up for you. You may be a single parent doing everything alone, trying to become better and do better yet life keeps getting in the way.

I understand.

That is why this book exists.

This book is your **blueprint** to motivate you, to help you keep going, to push you forward instead of backward. It is meant to help you press through when quitting feels easier.

Don't just read this book. **Take your time.**
Process my story as it can also help you overcome your story.

Take notes on what kept me going.
And then begin to figure out what will keep you going.

Because there is more inside of you that needs to be birthed.
More healing.
More purpose.
More life.

And this journey we're walking it together.

My Why and What Kept Me Going

What kept me going was my child. Even when life felt unbearable, even when I was rejected, broken, and alone, I knew I had to keep moving forward not for me, but for him.

I knew nobody would be able to love him the way I love him. I had to be stronger, rise again, and endure so he could live a life of joy, peace, and purpose. He didn't ask to be here, but God blessed me with a son......a son who gives me hope, a son who gives me strength, a son who encourages me even at just ten years old. He's smart. He's anointed and talented. And in his own way, he lifts me up when I feel down.

Even in my darkest moments, God used my son to remind me of His faithfulness. I remember a day when I was down to my last $20 and needed to buy diapers for him. I didn't have enough for the brand I usually buy. I walked up and down the aisle, wondering how I would make it work, looking for the cheapest brand, praying silently, God, I don't know what to do.

Then, an angel appeared literally. A stranger came up to me and handed me $20 while I was in the aisle for babies. She said she didn't know why, but God told her to bless me. I was able to buy the diapers I needed for my son. That moment wasn't just about money it was God's hand showing up in my life, proving he sees me, he provides, and he sustains.

And he didn't stop there. I remember wanting to feel good, look good, to take care of myself, but I didn't have the finances. I still wanted to treat myself to get my feet and nails done after a long day at work. God sent someone literally right next to me to pay for my nails at the salon, telling me to get whatever I wanted. I hadn't asked.... he just provided.

These moments taught me that even when I didn't know God fully, even when I felt abandoned, he was still there. He was still providing. He was still moving on my behalf. He used angels on assignments to help me, to remind me I wasn't alone, and to give me hope when I felt hopeless.

And, my dear reader, this is what kept me going. My son reminded me of my purpose, and God reminded me of His faithfulness. If He can do it for me, He can do it for you too. Even when your resources and finances are gone, even when doors are closed, even when life seems impossible God sees you. He knows your struggles. And He will provide.

God also made a way for me and my child in ways I could have never imagined. At the age of 20, I was looking for our first home as a first-time homebuyer, not knowing what I was doing. By the age of 21, we had moved into our very own home. I didn't have to fix a thing the house was ready for us.

I remember being told that I needed at least $3,000 in my savings account for a down payment. I had almost nothing.

But God… He made a way. I didn't have to put down a single dollar. I move into the home with Zero dollars down. I was amazed. I couldn't understand how it happened, but I knew it was God.

From that moment, my faith began to grow. I realized that God is real. God hears me. God sees me. He provides in ways that we often don't expect. Even the little things, like receiving help when I was down to my last.

Qualified by God, Not by People

Over the years, I've earned an honorary doctorate (Ph.D.) in Christian Leadership and Business. I am a prophet, motivational speaker, certified life coach, certified Youth Mental Health First Aid provider, author, business mentor, graphic designer, President of Thrive Girls, Inc., and CEO of Veda Consultants, LLC and Investments by Faith, LLC.

But the truth is **God Himself has been my greatest teacher**.

Along my journey, God sent prophets, pastors, preachers, mentors, coaches, and even strangers' people who poured into me for seasons and planted seeds I needed at the right time. God once told me, "I will send strangers to bless you and help you." **(Romans 12:13)**

If I'm being honest, sometimes I sabotaged the very help God sent. Because of the hurt I carried, I pushed people away. I could not always discern love from danger. Eventually, I had to repent and ask God to forgive me for rejecting what He sent to help me.

Rejected from the Womb

Before I even took my first breath, rejection was already part of my story.

My father told me stories, stories that I wish I had never heard. He told me that my mother had wanted an abortion. He said it right in front of both of us, and she confirmed it.

Yes, of course I did, she said and they both went on arguing back in forth about stories about how both parents really hurt and rejected me at some point.

Hearing that as a child broke me in ways I couldn't understand at the time. It explained the rejection I experienced from my mother later in life and the emotional unavailable father. It explained the coldness, the distance, and the feeling that I wasn't wanted even by the ones who brought me into this world.

I felt like a child pushed onto to my father expecting to navigate life without the nurturing, protection, or affirmation that I needed.

This early rejection set the tone for much of my life. It created wounds that I carried into relationships, school, family, and faith communities.

I didn't know then that God would meet me in those gaps, that his love would eventually remind me that I was chosen and deeply wanted.

Even when humanity rejected me, God never did. He saw me. He knew me. And He had a plan to turn my pain into my purpose.

When God's Promises Felt Impossible

Since I was a little girl, God would show me glimpses of what He planned to do in my life. He would speak promises over me, but I couldn't see how they would ever happen.

I didn't feel qualified.
I didn't feel smart enough.
I felt too broken.

I would get excited, then immediately discouraged. Yeah right, I would think. That can't be true.

Those were lies from the enemy curses I once spoke over myself that I later broke in the name of Jesus.

I am smart.
I am loved.
I can do all things through Christ who strengthens me.

Labeled Crazy, Built to Survive

People don't call me bold, independent, strong or even crazy for no reason.

What looks like confidence to some is actually survival.
What sounds unbelievable is simply what I endured and still got back up from.

What looks crazy to the world can be prophetic in the spirit.
There were moments I wanted to give up completely. Moments I wanted to throw in the towel, disappear, and stop fighting so hard just to exist. But God kept me.

He kept me because my life is not just about me.

I was created to help set people free. There is an entire bloodline connected to my obedience waiting on me to keep going, even when I'm tired, misunderstood, and rejected. There is a prophetic calling over my life that many in my bloodline don't understand. Some don't know how to support it. Some fear it. And some resent that it's me who carries the anointing.

But rejection does not cancel calling.

When God places an anointing on your life, it will often make others uncomfortable especially those closest to you. Not because you are doing something wrong, but because your obedience exposes what they've avoided, what they haven't healed from, or what they were never willing to confront.

I've been labeled "too much," "unstable," "dramatic," and "crazy." But what they called crazy was discernment. What they called weakness was endurance. What they called rebellion was obedience to God.

I survived things that should have broken me.
I endured things that should have silenced me.
And I kept going when giving up would have been easier.

Not because I was strong on my own but because God strengthened me.

Scriptures for the Misunderstood and Labeled

- 1 Corinthians 1:27 – "But God chose the foolish things of the world to shame the wise."
- Isaiah 54:17 – "No weapon formed against you shall prosper."

- 2 Corinthians 12:9 – "My grace is sufficient for you, for My power is made perfect in weakness."
- Genesis 50:20 – "What you meant for evil, God meant for good."

Declarations: Built to Survive

Speak or write these declarations:

1. I reject every false label spoken over my life.
2. I am not crazy, I am resilient, discerning, and called.
3. What I survived will serve someone else's healing.
4. I am anointed for this generation and my bloodline.
5. I will not shrink, silence myself, or dim my light to make others comfortable.

Reflection

- Have you ever been labeled or misunderstood for surviving?
- What parts of you were developed through pain, not privilege?
- What calling might God be protecting in you even through rejection?

Your Encouragement

If you've been labeled crazy, maybe it's because you survived what others couldn't.

If you've been misunderstood, maybe it's because you carry something others don't.

And if you're still standing after everything you've been through God is not finished with you yet.

You weren't built to break.

You were built to survive.

And your survival is someone else's hope.

Rejected Without a Support System

Life has a way of testing us at our weakest moments. Recently, I faced health challenges with an autoimmune disease that made every part of life harder. I lost my house. My car was stolen. I was a single parent doing everything on my own, with no backup, no safety net, and no one to lean on.

I reached out to my mother and grandmother, asking if my child and I could stay with them until I got back on my feet. Their answer was no. I even thought an aunt that I had would help me and my child. I was left to navigate this storm alone.

We stayed in hotels, moving from one place to another, trying to keep our lives afloat. I struggled to find a job that could accommodate my health, my child, and provide some stability. There was no support system. I had to do everything by myself.

It was lonely. It was depressing. There were nights when I didn't know what to do or where to turn. I had no family to go to. My child's father was absent from our lives, offering no mental, physical, or financial support. I couldn't even get child support because he wasn't working a w-2 form job. I reached out to other relatives, like my other aunt, and still, there was nothing.

And yet... I survived.

Through all of this, I learned something crucial: rejection can feel like the end, but sometimes it is God creating space for growth. It is God teaching you to rely fully on him. It is God showing you your own strength, resilience, and faith. Sometimes God wants to get the glory from our stories so we can know it was only him.

Even when no one else is there, God is there. Even when doors close, God opens new ones. Even when family turns away, God remains faithful.

This season taught me independence, faith, and resilience like nothing else ever could. I learned that life doesn't have to be easy to teach you how strong you really are.

Scriptures for Healing and Strength

- Isaiah 41:10 – "So do not fear, for I am with you; do not be dismayed, for I am your God. I will strengthen you and help you; I will uphold you with my righteous right hand."
- Psalm 68:5-6 – "A father to the fatherless, a defender of widows, is God in his holy dwelling. God sets the lonely in families."
- Deuteronomy 31:6 – "Be strong and courageous. Do not be afraid or terrified because of them, for the Lord your God goes with you; he will never leave you nor forsake you."

Declarations for Those Without Support

1. I am not alone; God is my ultimate support and protector.
2. I release every fear, loneliness, and anxiety into God's hands.
3. I am strong, resilient, and capable of overcoming every obstacle.
4. I will rise above rejection and live in purpose and faith.
5. I trust God to provide guidance, peace, and provision in every situation.

Reflection

- Where in my life do I feel unsupported or alone?
- How can I invite God's presence into these areas to provide comfort and strength?
- What steps can I take to walk forward in faith, knowing God is my refuge and my help?

Remember, being without a support system doesn't mean being without help. It's an opportunity to **lean deeper into God, discover your own strength, and grow in faith**. The challenges you face today will become the testimonies that inspire and encourage others tomorrow.

Rejected by Siblings

Some of the deepest rejections I have experienced came from my own family, my siblings.

I was told I wouldn't amount to anything. I was told I would be like "the rest of the Walkers." I was told I wouldn't pass my tests. Words of death were spoken over me instead of life. Words meant to discourage, disqualify, and define me.

But God spoke the opposite:
"I will live and not die and declare the works of the Lord." **(Psalm 118:17)**
"For I know the plans I have for you..." **(Jeremiah 29:11)**
"Now unto to him that is able to do exceedingly above all things that we ask or think, according to the power working in us" **(Ephesians 3:20)**

Like Joseph in the Bible, my siblings were jealous of me. They resented the way I was treated differently, even though I never compared our lives. I never measured whose life was better or worse but they did. I simply knew we had all endured trauma in different ways, and each of our paths was unique and different.

Jealousy wasn't just about material things or opportunities, it was about acceptance, love, and acknowledgment.

They didn't like that I was chosen differently, or that I walked a path that was mine alone. Their envy, anger, and bitterness eventually turned into witchcraft and my life became another form of rejection I had to endure.

Even today, my siblings struggle with jealousy, hate, pride, lies and more. They don't really support me. They don't show up for me or even my child (Their Nephew) That rejection cuts deeply, because family is supposed to be our safe place the people who should love, encourage, and stand by us no matter what.

But through it all, God's voice became louder than theirs. He reminded me that their rejection does not determine my worth or my destiny. Their words cannot nullify God's plan over my life.

Healing Scriptures

- "Do not let any unwholesome talk come out of your mouths, but only what is helpful for building others up according to their needs, that it may benefit those who listen." (Ephesians 4:29)
- "Bless those who curse you, pray for those who mistreat you."(Luke 6:28)
- "Though my father and mother forsake me, the Lord will receive me." (Psalm 27:10)

Declarations for Healing from Sibling Rejection

1. I am not defined by my siblings/family' words or actions.
2. I release every hurt, every judgment, and every envy into God's hands.
3. I declare favor, success, and peace over my life.
4. I forgive those who have rejected me, and I am free from bitterness.
5. I walk in God's purpose, regardless of who supports or rejects me.

Reflection

Take a moment to consider:

- Are there family members who have rejected or hurt me?
- How has that affected my self-worth and my path?
- What does God want me to learn about His love and my value in Him?

Even when siblings, parents, or loved ones reject us, God's love remains constant. Your destiny is not determined by their acceptance it is determined by God's purpose for your life.

Rejected in the House of God—Protected by God

When I walked into the church, I was searching for refuge. I came looking for love, support, and community the things we are taught the church represents. I believed I would be welcomed with open arms, covered in prayer, and surrounded by people who would walk with me as I healed.

Instead, I was rejected.

I remember a leader questioning: Why am I here? I'm supposed to dress a certain way etc.

It started to make me feel like I didn't belong. The very place I thought would help me heal became another source of pain, confusion, and grief.

At the time, I didn't understand it.

I didn't realize that what felt like rejection was actually God's protection.

I didn't know that staying in that environment would have pulled me deeper into warfare more hurt, more spiritual confusion, more rejection layered on top of wounds I was already carrying.

I went in looking for support, but God saw what I couldn't see. He knew that not every church is safe for every season, and not every door labeled "God" is where He wants you to stay.

That rejection hurt deeply, especially because it came from people who claimed to represent God. But God is not confined to a building, and He does not always move through institutions the way we expect Him to.

Sometimes God removes you quietly.
Sometimes He allows rejection to speak louder than a warning ever could.

I later realized that if I had been embraced in that place, I might have stayed somewhere that would have delayed my healing, distorted my identity, and intensified my pain. God loved me enough to block access even when it hurt.

Church hurt can make you question God, but I learned that God was never the one rejecting me. He was the one rescuing me.

If you've ever been hurt, ignored, dismissed, unseen, or pushed out of a church while genuinely seeking help, know this: it does not mean you were unworthy. It does not mean you lacked faith. And it does not mean God turned His back on you.

Sometimes rejection is redirection.
Sometimes rejection is protection.
And sometimes God will remove you from a place simply because He has something better and safer for you.

That experience taught me that my relationship with God is personal. It is not dependent on approval, titles, or acceptance from people. God knew me there, just as He knows me now.

And He was with me even when the people in the church wasn't.

Discouraged, But Still Favored

When I attended medical assistant school, my own brother told me I wouldn't pass. He said my school wasn't a real school because it was a trade school. He said I wouldn't get a job because one of his friends went to school for the same thing and had a hard time finding jobs in that field.

I believed him.

When test day came, I failed by 30 points.

I was crushed. But God still gave me favor. My school allowed me to walk in graduation, receive credits, and retake the exam. And despite everything spoken against me, God opened doors for me to work with doctors and hospitals as a Medical Assistant without the certification.
Rejection did not cancel favor.

Scriptures for Discouragement and Favor

- Isaiah 54:17 – "No weapon formed against you shall prosper, and every tongue which rises against you in judgment you shall condemn."
- Proverbs 16:7 – "When a man's ways please the Lord, He makes even his enemies to be at peace with him."
- Psalm 84:11 – "For the Lord God is a sun and shield; the Lord bestows favor and honor. No good thing does He withhold from those who walk uprightly."

Declarations: Still Favored

Speak these aloud or write them:

1. I reject every word spoken against my success and ability.
2. Even when I fall short, God's favor goes before me and opens doors.
3. Failure is not my final outcome, God's grace rewrites my story.
4. I am qualified by God, not limited by people's opinions.

Your Encouragement

If you've ever been discouraged by the words of someone close to you especially someone who should have supported, you know this: their doubt does not override God's plan. A setback does not mean you are disqualified. God's favor can meet you even in moments of failure and open doors you didn't think were possible.

What people speak over you does not determine your outcome God does.
Rejection did not cancel your calling.
Discouragement did not cancel your destiny.
And failure did not cancel God's favor over your life.

If God did it for me, He can do it for you too.

Dreams Deferred and Wrong Turns

Before that, I worked at Amazon trying to figure out my purpose. I had my child at nineteen. I wanted to go to trucking school, but my father discouraged me because he didn't pass.

So, I stopped believing I could.

I worked in other departments driving forklifts, loading trucks, and making deliveries. My body began to break down from a car accident I had back issues and a herniated disc. I was tired physically, emotionally, spiritually.

I once dreamed of cosmetology, fashion, massage therapy, owning a spa but I didn't have the resources, finances or support system to guide me. I gave up and went down the wrong path, dating the wrong men and searching for love in broken places.

Scriptures for Dreams Deferred and Redirection

- Proverbs 13:12 – "Hope deferred makes the heart sick, but a longing fulfilled is a tree of life."
- Jeremiah 29:11 – "For I know the plans I have for you," declares the Lord, "plans to prosper you and not to harm you, plans to give you hope and a future."
- Romans 8:28 – "And we know that in all things God works for the good of those who love Him, who have been called according to His purpose."

Declarations: Restored Dreams

Speak or write these declarations:

1. I release every dream I abandoned due to fear, lack, or discouragement.
2. Even detours and wrong turns are being redeemed by God.
3. My future is not limited by my past decisions or delayed beginnings.
4. God is restoring my purpose, strength, and vision for my life.

Your Encouragement

Dreams deferred can make you feel stuck, tired, and unsure of who you are or where you're going. When support is missing and resources are limited, it's easy to give up on what once inspired you and settle for survival instead of purpose.

But hear this: delayed does not mean denied. Wrong turns do not cancel God's calling. Even seasons of exhaustion, injury, and disappointment can become part of the process God uses to redirect you not to destroy you.

If you've ever stopped believing in yourself because someone else couldn't see your potential, know that God still sees it. He is not finished with you. He is restoring what you laid down in survival mode, and He is leading you back to purpose stronger, wiser, and more aware than before.

Your dreams may have paused, but they are not dead.

A Toxic Home and a Wounded Heart

As a child, I grew up in a toxic environment constantly arguing, fighting, breaking up, and getting back together. No one realized how deeply it affected me.

I followed my father's past for a moment unknowingly I dated emotional unavailable men just like him believing love would save me. But trauma follows you when it is not healed and it eventually repeats itself if you don't get to the root of it.

Also, my own siblings didn't support me. I was the only child of my father. As we got older, things shifted. One day I asked my brother why he treats me different and why he don't really talk to me like he talks to my older sister.... even though there is an age gap he told me, "You're not my full sister. You're my half-sister."

That hurt deeply.

Scriptures for Healing from a Toxic Home and Wounded Relationships

- Psalm 34:18 – "The Lord is close to the brokenhearted and saves those who are crushed in spirit."
- Isaiah 61:1 – "He has sent Me to bind up the brokenhearted, to proclaim freedom for the captives and release from darkness for the prisoners."
- Psalm 27:10 – "Though my father and mother forsake me, the Lord will receive me."

Declarations: Healing the Wounded Heart

Speak or write these declarations:

1. I am not defined by the environment I grew up in.
2. I break unhealthy relationship patterns rooted in unhealed trauma.
3. God is healing my heart and teaching me what healthy love looks like.
4. I am accepted, valued, and chosen by God even when people reject me.

Your Encouragement

Growing up in a toxic home can shape how you see love, safety, and relationships. When chaos becomes normal, we often carry those patterns into adulthood believing love means enduring pain or proving our worth to people who cannot give us what we need.

But God wants you to know this: your wounds are not your identity. Trauma may explain your choices, but it does not have to define your future. Healing begins when you acknowledge the pain, invite God into it, and choose to break the cycle.

If you've ever felt rejected by family, misunderstood by siblings, or wounded by words that cut deep, know that God's acceptance is greater than human rejection.

He is restoring your heart, redefining love for you, and calling you into relationships rooted in peace, safety, and truth.

You are not too broken to heal.
You are not too wounded to be loved.
And you are not alone on this journey.

Forced to Grow Up Too Soon

I grew up faster than I was supposed to. At ten years old, my innocence was taken by a family member. I was bullied in school and traumatized in silence.

By seventeen, I experienced pregnancy and miscarriage. By eighteen, I was pregnant again still searching for safety, love, and from my child's father.

Trauma stacked on trauma.

I experienced betrayal, fear, anxiety, threats to my life, and deep emotional wounds. I experienced depression and a mental breakdown not because I was broken, but because too much had happened to me.

Scriptures for Those Forced to Grow Up Too Soon

- Psalm 147:3 – "He heals the brokenhearted and binds up their wounds."
- Joel 2:25 – "I will restore to you the years that the locust has eaten."
- Isaiah 43:2 – "When you pass through the waters, I will be with you... When you walk through the fire, you will not be burned."

Declarations: Restoring What Was Taken

Speak or write these declarations:

1. What was taken from me does not define me, God is restoring me.
2. I am not weak because I broke; I broke because I carried too much.
3. God is healing my inner child and redeeming my lost years.
4. My story will not end in trauma, but in triumph and purpose.

Your Encouragement

Being forced to grow up too soon leaves invisible wounds that many people never see. When innocence is stolen, trauma compounds, and pain is silenced, the weight becomes unbearable. Depression, anxiety, and breakdowns are not signs of weakness; they are signs that your soul has been overloaded for too long.

Hear this clearly: you were not broken you were burdened. You were not fragile you were surviving.

God saw every tear, every betrayal, every moment you were searching for safety and love. Even when you didn't have the words to cry out, He was there. And though trauma may have shaped parts of your journey, it does not get to define your ending.

If you've ever felt like too much happened too soon...
If you've ever felt robbed of childhood, peace, or safety...
God is still able to restore what trauma tried to destroy.
You are still here for a reason.
Your survival is proof of purpose.
And your healing will become someone else's hope.

Betrayed by Blood

Some of the deepest wounds I carry did not come from strangers.
They came from people who were supposed to protect me.

I was financially taken advantage of. I was falsely accused. Lies were spoken about my character, my mental health, and my ability as a mother. I was isolated, judged, and left for dead to defend myself with no support.

I was left to survive alone.

What hurt the most was realizing that my own family members turned against me. Instead of covering me, they rejected me. Instead of protecting me, they participated in the harm. Some of them communicated with my ex behind my back. Some believed lies without ever asking me the truth. Others watched me struggle and chose silence and gossip.

That kind of betrayal cuts deep because blood is supposed to be safe.

God even began to reveal things to me spiritually things I didn't want to see.

I became aware that jealousy, resentment, and spiritual opposition were at work. I saw how envy can twist hearts and how unresolved pain can turn people against the very one who is trying to break cycles and heal.

Not everyone celebrates the one who chooses growth.
Not everyone supports the one who refuses to stay bound.

I learned that sometimes betrayal isn't personal, it's spiritual. When God places a calling on your life, when you carry light, when you choose healing, it exposes darkness in others. And exposure often brings resistance.

But hear this: betrayal did not destroy me.

I survived the lies.
I survived the abandonment.
I survived being misunderstood and misrepresented.

And I survived because God was with me.

What people tried to use to break me, God used to reveal truth. What they meant to isolate me, God used to strengthen me. What they meant to silence me, God used to sharpen my discernment.

I learned that family does not always mean alignment. Blood does not always mean loyalty. And access does not always mean assignment.

God had to remove people even relatives so He could protect me, heal me, and prepare me for what was ahead.
And although the betrayal hurt deeply, it did not get the final word.

Scriptures for Betrayal, Healing, and God's Justice

- Psalm 55:12–14 – "If an enemy were insulting me, I could endure it... but it is you, a close companion."
- Micah 7:6–7 – "A man's enemies are the members of his own household... But as for me, I watch in hope for the Lord."
- Psalm 34:18 – "The Lord is close to the brokenhearted and saves those who are crushed in spirit."
- Romans 12:19 – "Do not avenge yourselves... for it is written: 'Vengeance is Mine, says the Lord.'"
- Genesis 50:20 – "What you meant for evil, God meant for good."

Declarations: Healing from Betrayal

1. I release the pain of betrayal and choose healing.
2. I am no longer bound to the actions or intentions of others.
3. God is my defender, my vindicator, and my protector.
4. What was done in secret is being healed in truth.
5. I forgive to free myself not to excuse what happened.

Reflection

- Have you experienced betrayal from people you trusted or loved?
- How has that betrayal affected your ability to trust or feel safe?
- What would it look like to allow God to heal those wounds, one layer at a time?

Your Encouragement

If you were betrayed by blood, know this:
God sees it. God knows it. And God is not finished with you.
Betrayal may have wounded you, but it did not define you.
Isolation may have hurt you, but it did not end you.
You are still here.
You are still standing.
And you are still chosen.

Breaking Generational Chains

My warfare has been intense because I am not only healing, I am breaking generational cycles and coming from a bloodline that operated in witchcraft.

I am exposing dysfunction, silence, trauma, and spiritual bondage that existed long before me. Patterns that were passed down, normalized, and never addressed. Cycles of rejection, abuse, poverty, abandonment, fear, and pain that tried to follow me into adulthood.

What the enemy meant to destroy me, God used to awaken me.

Many people don't understand what spiritual warfare is. Warfare isn't always loud. Sometimes it looks like exhaustion. Sometimes it feels like repeated loss, rejection, confusion, and isolation. Sometimes it shows up as attacks on your mind, your family, your finances, your health, and your identity all at once.

You are often attacked the most in the very area you are assigned to break.

When God calls you to dismantle generational cycles, you don't just deal with your own pain you feel the weight of what others refused to heal. You stand in the gap for bloodlines that never had the courage, awareness, or support to change. You disrupt what was comfortable. You expose what was hidden. And that kind of assignment can come with resistance.

Breaking generational chains is not easy.

There were moments I wanted to give up. Moments I questioned why my life felt so hard when I was trying to do right. Moments I asked God, “Why me?” But deep down, I knew I could not afford to keep living in cycles that kept producing pain.

I wanted different.
I wanted more.
And I deserved better and greater.

So, I chose healing, even when it hurt.
I chose truth, even when it cost me relationships.
I chose obedience, even when it felt lonely.

Because someone had to say, “It stops here.”
And that someone was me.

Scriptures on Generational Healing & Warfare

- Galatians 3:13 – “Christ has redeemed us from the curse of the law, being made a curse for us.”
- Ezekiel 18:2–3 – “The soul who sins shall die... You will no longer quote this proverb in Israel.”
- 2 Corinthians 10:3–5 – “For though we live in the world, we do not wage war as the world does...”
- Isaiah 61:7 – “Instead of your shame you will receive a double portion.”
- Joel 2:25 – “I will restore to you the years the locust has eaten.”

Declarations: Breaking Generational Chains

1. I am the cycle breaker in my bloodline.
2. What bound my family will not bind me or my children.
3. I reject every generational curse and receive God's freedom.
4. I choose healing over silence and truth over denial.
5. God is restoring what was lost and multiplying what was stolen.
6. I am not cursed I am called, chosen, and covered by God.

Reflection

Take time with these questions:

- What patterns do I see repeating in my family or life?
- What behaviors, beliefs, or cycles do I want to stop with me?
- What would healing look like for my future and my children?
- Am I willing to do the uncomfortable work to create change?

Encouragement

If your life feels harder than others, it may be because your assignment is heavier. But hear this: **God never assigns what He doesn't empower.**

You are not being punished, you are being prepared.

The chains break with you.
The healing begins with you.
And the freedom will flow through you.

Left for Dead, But Kept by God

I share this part of my story to remind you that you are not alone.

I admitted myself into a mental hospital at one of the lowest points of my life with assistance from a pastor I shared my trauma, warfare, and things I've been experiencing since leaving one church to her church and I didn't understand it. She told me she was a mess leaving the same church I did and her daughter experienced a lot similar to me and believe this facility would help me since they helped her daughter too. She told me this facility had nurses and therapist onsite I could see and speak with immediately and at first I was not aware it was a mental hospital but I sill assist on going because I just wanted some type of help. It felt like I had been left for dead.

The only thing that kept me alive mentally, emotionally, and spiritually was my Bible. I thank God that my father spoke up and made sure I had it, because without the Word of God, I truly don't know how I would have survived. The doctor assigned to me only spoke to me one time and when I started talking about God and spiritual warfare he got upset asking if I think I could hear God and I said yes and he giggled. After that, he spoke more to my mother than to me.

"Your mom said this."
"Your mom said that."

“Your mom says you’re crazy.”
“Your mom says you need medication.” and etc.

My voice didn’t matter.
My truth didn’t matter.

To make matters worse, I had COVID, so I was isolated in a room by myself. No windows. Just a dark room with a bed, a shower, and a toilet. It felt like jail. Night after night, I was alone with my thoughts, my trauma, and my fear.

They told me I needed to be on medication. When I asked why, they said I had schizophrenia and my mom
kept calling them to tell them lies and said I was crazy. I didn’t understand how they came to that conclusion. Something didn’t sit right in my spirit.

I was given a phone, and I stayed in contact with my dad. I also called my cousin and gave her the names of the medications they were giving me so she could look them up. What alarmed me was that during the night shift, the medications were different five or six pills that didn’t match what I had been told.

At first, when I took the medication, I began to feel dizzy, lightheaded, and nauseous. It felt like I wasn’t going to wake up. One night, a nurse had to shake me repeatedly, saying, “Wake up, wake up time to take more medicine.” That’s when I heard the Holy Spirit clearly say, “Don’t take it.”

After that, I stopped swallowing the medication. I would hide it in my Bible or place it under my tongue because they were watching me. When I asked a nurse for the list of medications, she wrote it down and handed it to me.

I told her it was completely different from what they were giving me at night. She said she didn't know what I was talking about.

I couldn't sleep. I tossed and turned, feeling deep in my spirit That something was off. Around 10 p.m. one night, I asked to use the phone to call my family so they could pick me up. I told them this wasn't the place for me. This wasn't what I expected when I came there for help.

What led me there hurts just as much. When I realized this was not the place for me, I tried to leave on my own.

I had checked myself into the facility with assistants from a so I believed I had the right to check myself out. When I told them I wanted to leave, they said no. That didn't make sense to me. Fear began to rise in my spirit and anger.

In desperation, I attempted to let myself out by scanning a staff badge. The staff punched me the back of my head. The moment I did, everything escalated. Staff members rushed me all at once. Voices were raised. I felt surrounded, overwhelmed, and attacked.

I told her it was completely different from what they were giving me at night. She said she didn't know what I was talking about.

I couldn't sleep. I tossed and turned, feeling deep in my spirit That something was off. Around 10 p.m. one night, I asked to use the phone to call my family so they could pick me up. I told them this wasn't the place for me. This wasn't what I expected when I came there for help.

What led me there hurts just as much. When I realized this was not the place for me, I tried to leave on my own.

I had checked myself into the facility with assistants from a so I believed I had the right to check myself out. When I told them I wanted to leave, they said no. That didn't make sense to me. Fear began to rise in my spirit and anger.

In desperation, I attempted to let myself out by scanning a staff badge. The staff punched me the back of my head. The moment I did, everything escalated. Staff members rushed me all at once. Voices were raised. I felt surrounded, overwhelmed, and attacked.

In that moment, I heard the Holy Spirit clearly say, "Stop. Before you make it worse for yourself."
I froze and apologized and let them know the reason why I did this.

I realized then that this was bigger than what I could fight in my own strength.

In that moment, I heard the Holy Spirit clearly say, "Stop. Before you make it worse for yourself."
I froze and apologized and let them know the reason why I did this.

I realized then that this was bigger than what I could fight in my own strength.

I wasn't being protected, nobody wanted to listen to me, I was being restrained. They were determined to keep me in that facility and keep me medicated, even though something in my spirit told me this wasn't right. remember walking out my room into the hallway crying just kept calling on Jesus. "Jesus, Jesus Jesus". I noticed other patients in their rooms begin to walk out the hallway and the staff told me to be quiet he won't save me. I was in shocked and said you will see. I continued to call Jesus name and two elder ladies began to speak out loud saying she don't know why she even came to this facility she just has a drug addiction and she wants help. Another elder lady said she only came here because she been feeling depressed nobody wants to help her. A guy name Matthew came out and said he come here all time to get drugged due to him getting himself in a drug cult and don't know how to get out. I begin to read my bible we were all forced to get back in our rooms to go to bed. I had to get an attorney involved to get out.

It took legal intervention for me to be released from a place I voluntarily entered seeking help. A place that was supposed to bring healing instead became another place of bondage. But even there, God was watching over me. Even there, He was guiding me when to stop, when to be still, and how to get out safely.

What the enemy meant to trap me, God used to teach me discernment.

Part of the emotional break down that had led me to the mental hospital was a pastor from a church I had attended who had already rejected me once encouraged me to go to this facility.

She said it helped her daughter and promised that if I felt uncomfortable, call her and say the word “butterfly” and she will pick me up.

But while I sat in the lobby with her and both my parents waiting with me to be checked in, the warfare intensified and I didn’t understand where and why this attack was so heavy.

The pastor had to leave urgently saying her daughter called, saying a group of girls were following her, trying to fight her. The things that started happening to her child mirrored things that had happened to me in my childhood.

I’ve had experienced that same situation before. Yet when I was in the facility, the pastor never checked on me. She never answered her phone. That rejection cut deeply.

My mother had given the pastor my dog to take care of which was also upsetting at the moment, but I didn't have no one to else to care for my dog at the time. When I was finally released from the mental hospital facility with the help of an attorney, there were so many lies going back and forth within my family that I didn't know who to trust. She also, took my car and my keys, while my father was trying to step in and help in different ways, but it was so much confusion. When I eventually got my car back, there was a strong odor inside my car, as if something had been sprayed that could knock someone out. I couldn't drive it, so my father had to help me get the car cleaned out.

As I walked upstairs in my home, I noticed that the same strong odor that was in my car was throughout the upstairs of my home. I asked my mother what she had sprayed in my house, since she was the only person who had access to my personal belongings and been in my house. She responded by saying she didn't know what I was talking about and acted unaware.

My father helped me open all the windows so the house could air out, and I had to stay at his home for a few weeks because of the situation. Later, pastors and prophets discerned the warfare surrounding me and confirmed things my mother was doing was operating out of witchcraft, manipulation, and what I experienced was not of God.

They warned me to be cautious, saying they sensed jealousy, spiritual opposition, and harmful intentions. Not only that but the pastor and church I went to operate as a cult but also reassured me that I would live and that God was protecting me.

Before all of this, I had already left another church. I felt God telling me it was time to leave. I prayed and said, "God, if this is You, have her give me the microphone and I I'll honor her and say my goodbyes." She did. She said, "Veda, God says you have something to say." I thanked her and told the congregation that God told me to leave. But suddenly, she stopped me, took the mic, and said, "It's not your time to go. God didn't say that." She laid hands on me and pushed me, and I fell to the floor as if the Holy Spirit had done it.

I was confused and emotionally broken.

How could she say God told her I had something to say and then say I wasn't hearing Him? One moment I was considered powerful and anointed, and the next moment, when it was time for me to leave, it wasn't God anymore.

That confusion opened the door to mental warfare I didn't understand.

My family turned against me. My mind was under attack.

My home, my child, my finances, everything was shaken at once. I didn't know what was happening. I stayed in a hotel praying, crying out for help, asking people to help me understand.

One prophet told me I was under spiritual attack and prayed for me, but the warfare continued. I went to an old church member's home, and they gave me scriptures to read.

I went to another church, and a woman shared how she had gone through similar pain after leaving the same church. She tried to help me. But the warfare didn't stop because I didn't know how to really pray at the time. I didn't know what scriptures to read at the time. I didn't know where to start in the Bible.

Everything I had seen focused on laying hands and casting out demons. I had never experienced anything like that before. It scared me. No one taught me about healing, discipleship, demonic spirits or deliverance without understanding.

But even in all of that confusion, God kept me.
I should not be here.

But I am.

And that is proof that God knows me.
And He knows you too.

Scriptures for Those Who Have Been Misunderstood, Misdiagnosed, or Spiritually Confused:

- Psalm 34:19 – "Many are the afflictions of the righteous, but the Lord delivers him out of them all."
- Isaiah 43:2 – "When you pass through the waters, I will be with you."
- John 10:27 – "My sheep hear My voice, and I know them, and they follow Me."
- Psalm 118:17 – "I will live and not die, and declare the works of the Lord."

• 2 Timothy 1:7 – "For God has not given us a spirit of fear, but of power, love, and a sound mind."

Declarations of Healing & Discernment
Speak these aloud:

1. I am not abandoned I am kept by God.
2. My mind is sound, protected, and renewed.
3. I discern God's voice clearly and confidently.
4. What tried to break me will not define me.
5. I am healed, whole, and covered by God's truth.

Reflection

- Have you ever been misunderstood in a place you went to for help?
- Where has confusion entered your faith or identity?
- What would it look like to trust God's voice again, gently and safely?

Truth

Rejection does not mean God has left you.
Confusion does not mean you are broken.
Isolation does not mean you are forgotten.

Sometimes it means God is preserving you for a deeper healing.

And if you are still here so is your purpose.

Through all of the pain, confusion, and rejection, I learned one powerful truth: **God is always with you, even when people fail, even when institutions fail, even when the world rejects you.**

Rejection hurts. It shakes your soul, makes you question your worth, and can leave you feeling alone. But rejection does not define you God defines you. The Word of God reminds us:

- Psalm 34:18 – "The Lord is close to the brokenhearted and saves those who are crushed in spirit."
- Isaiah 41:10 – "So do not fear, for I am with you; do not be dismayed, for I am your God. I will strengthen you and help you; I will uphold you with my righteous right hand."
- Psalm 27:10 – "Though my father and mother forsake me, the Lord will receive me."

Even when the world says "you don't belong", God says "You are mine. You are chosen. You are loved."

Take a moment to reflect on these questions:

- Where have I experienced rejection in my life?
- How have I allowed those experiences to define me?
- How can I invite God into those moments to bring healing and restoration?

____

____

____

____

When the Battle Is in the Bloodline

I didn't understand most of the things I was going through at the time.
I didn't understand the attacks.
I didn't understand the warfare.
I just knew I was fighting something deeper than people; something tied to my bloodline.

I could see patterns on both my mother's side and my father's side. Cycles of hurt, jealousy, control, and brokenness that had never been healed, only repeated. I didn't have the language for it then, but I knew I was dealing with spiritual warfare rooted in generations.

At one point, I forgave my mother and tried again. After she read my first book, we talked, and for a moment, I thought things would change. I spoke life over her. I chose forgiveness. I decided to love her where she was while accepting where I was with God. I created boundaries not out of bitterness, but out of wisdom.

I realized she may not be able to love me the way I needed. Not because she didn't want to, but because her own childhood wounds were never healed. Hurt people hurt people, and cycles continue until someone decides to break them. I pray for my mother's healing daily. I love her, but I hate the jealousy, resentment, and unspoken anger.

So, I ask God daily to forgive me and help me forgive both of my parents.

I still don't fully understand why my relationships with them are so broken. I wish things were different. I wish they would change.

Unexpectedly, I became sick.

I was diagnosed with autoimmune disease I didn't see coming but it felt like others did. It was as if things were seen before I even moved, and opposition rose before I acted. Before I ever decided to move to another state, I remember going to my mother's house when she and my sister began asking strange questions:
"What state do you live in?"
"What insurance do you have?"
"What hospitals do you go to?"

At the time, I was still living in Delaware. I didn't understand why they were asking. Later, God whispered to me, "It's time for you to move."

I didn't know where I was going. I didn't have a plan. I just obeyed.
I moved to Texas.

Shortly after moving, I got sick. I went back to my mother, hoping again that things would be different.

She helped me at first. She took me to appointments. She took me to doctors. And then she asked me when I was leaving.
I told her I wasn't fully healed yet. I still had fluid in my lungs. The doctor said I couldn't fly in a plane yet. Her response broke me.

"You can't stay here."

I didn't know what to do. I was nervous about the government shutdown. I needed another procedure. I had no place to go. My insurance was still registered in Delaware. I hadn't fully transitioned to Texas. I wasn't expecting to get sick or to deal with mold issues in my home. I was a single parent, sick, displaced, and overwhelmed.

I went through procedures alone.
No visits.
No check-ins.
No calls.

Only my grandmother came.

I went back for another procedure, still fluid in my lungs. Still, no one checked on me. I stayed with my other grandmother. My dad took me to appointments. And in the middle of all of this, I felt the deepest rejection I've ever known.

Rejected while sick.
Rejected while homeless.

Rejected while unemployed.
Rejected while caring for a child alone.

My sister was allowed to stay. I was not.

It hurt. It still hurts.

I thought the church would be different. I thought I had support there. But when I needed them most, almost no one showed up except 2-3 people who I believe genuinely checked on me.

Sometimes rejection pushed me back toward the same people who hurt me, hoping they would change. But God showed me something hard: I had to be the one to change, not just for me, but for my child.

My calling is heavier because the warfare is deeper.
The hatred, jealousy, envy, and spiritual opposition running through my bloodline stops with me.

Even in the middle of sickness...
Even in homelessness...
Even in unemployment...
I said, "God, I trust You."
I don't always understand my story, but I trust the Author.

Scriptures: When the Battle Is in the Bloodline

- Exodus 20:5–6 – "...but showing love to a thousand generations of those who love Me and keep My commandments."
- Isaiah 59:19 – "When the enemy comes in like a flood, the Spirit of the Lord will lift up a standard against him."
- Galatians 3:13 – "Christ redeemed us from the curse of the law by becoming a curse for us."

Declarations: Breaking Generational Cycles

1. I am the cycle-breaker God chose for my bloodline.
2. Every generational curse stops with me and will not touch my child.
3. I choose boundaries, healing, and obedience over guilt and fear.
4. What rejected me will not follow me into my future.

Encouragement

Sometimes the hardest battles don't come from strangers, they come from family. When the warfare is in the bloodline, separation feels painful, confusing, and lonely. But distance is not dishonor, and boundaries are not rejection, they are protection.

If you've been rejected in your weakest moments...
If you've trusted God while sick, homeless, or alone...
If you've felt misunderstood, unsupported, and unseen...

Know this: God chose you to break what others refused to heal.

The battle is heavy because your assignment is powerful.
The resistance is strong because your purpose is dangerous to the enemy.
And the rejection hurts because you were never meant to stay bound there.
You are not abandoned.
You are being set apart.
And what runs in your bloodline ends with you.

Write down your thoughts, pray, and ask God to show you **what He wants you to learn from rejection**, because every pain carries a purpose when placed in His hands.

____

____

____

____

____

____

____

____

____

____

____

____

____

Remember, rejection can be protection, redirection, and even a sign that God is preparing you for something greater. Like He did for me, God will carry you through the storms, guide you through the confusion, and bring you into places of peace, purpose, and restoration.

Even in the darkest places, you are not alone. God knows you. God sees you. And His love will never fail.

You're Not Rejected, But You're Chosen

Thank you.
Thank you for taking the time to read my story.
Thank you for allowing me into your heart, your space, and your journey through this book, "Rejected But Chosen."

My prayer is that these pages touched you in the exact places you needed healing. That they reached your heart, your mind, your soul, and even your body. I pray that as you read, God began to reveal things, mend broken places, and restore areas you may have buried or avoided for years.

I pray that you heal from what hurt you.
I pray that you learn what you needed to learn.
I pray that you break cycles you were never meant to repeat.
And I pray that you walk boldly into the places God has already ordained for you to go, so you can obtain everything He has already ordained for you to have.

If you take nothing else from my story, take this truth with you:
You are not rejected. You are chosen.
You were chosen for such a time as this.

God chose you to walk through the fire not because He wanted to harm you, but because He knew you would survive it. He knew He could trust you with it. He knew you would come out refined, not destroyed. He knew you would carry the wisdom, strength, compassion, and authority needed to help others who would one day walk a similar path.

People may have rejected you.
They may have misunderstood you.
They may have walked away, spoken against you, or failed to support you.

But **God chose you.**

God loves you.
He does not hate you.
He does not dislike you.
He does not regret creating you.

He sees you.
He honors you.
He values you.
And He is proud of you for surviving what should have broken you.

Every tear you cried mattered.
Every prayer you whispered was heard.
Every lonely night was seen.
And every step you took forward even when you were tired was counted.

Rejection was not the end of your story.
It was the training ground.

It was the pruning.
It was the preparation.

You were never abandoned.
You were being positioned.

As you close this book, I want you to walk away knowing this:
Your life has purpose.
Your pain has meaning.
And your survival is not accidental.

You are still here because God is not finished with you.

I give all thanks, honor, and glory to God for carrying me and for meeting you right where you are.

In Jesus' name,
Amen.

About The Author

Dr. NAVEDA WALKER, also known *as "Coach Veda,"* is a single mother, certified life coach, certified youth mental health first aid, and motivational speaker dedicated to empowering individuals and guiding them towards transformative healing and their God-ordained purpose.

As Executive Director, founder. and coach of Thrive Girls Inc nonprofit organization, she passionately uplifts and supports young women, drawing from her own experiences to inspire and empower them. Through teachings, prayers, she impacts lives, providing a guiding light and imparting wisdom for positive transformation.

As CEO of Veda Consultants LLC and Investments By Faith LLC, a consultant and graphic designing company, she combines her creative skills and coaching passion to help individuals navigate life and business in various areas. Driven by love and concern for the next generation. She promotes self-worth, and fosters self-love, equipping them with tools, encouragement, and inspiration. With unwavering dedication, wisdom, and passion, Coach Veda stands as a beacon of hope, ready to guide you towards a life of healing, purpose, and self-empowerment.

contact me

BOOK DR. NAVEDA WALKER TODAY!

Social Media: YouTube
*@ThriveGirlsInc | @InvestementsByFaith | @VedaWalker_*

Websites:
(Nonprofit) www.ThriveGirlsInc.org
(Coaching) www.VedaWalker.com
(Business Consulting) www.InvestmentsByFaith.com

Speaking Engagements or Workshops:
Email - *info@ThriveGirlsInc.org*

FOLLOW ME

www.ThriveGirlsInc.org

www.VedaWalker.com

Management & consulting

www.InvestmentsByFaith.com

www.ingramcontent.com/pod-product-compliance
Lightning Source LLC
LaVergne TN
LVHW050609100826
845148LV00015B/3199

* 9 7 9 8 2 3 4 0 4 4 4 7 1 *